Stubborn Heart

New Poems

Clifton Snider

Sheila-Na-Gig Editions
Volume 10

Author photo: Deborah Snider
Cover art: Janet Lynn Higley

ISBN: 978-1-7354002-5-9
Library of Congress Control Number: 2021940222

Published by Sheila-Na-Gig Editions
Russell, KY
Hayley Mitchell Haugen, Editor
www.sheilanagigblog.com

Acknowledgments

Some of these poems have appeared in the following publications, sometimes in different forms. I am grateful to the editors and publishers.

Cadence Collective (cadencecollective.net): "Orlando," "Synchronicity," "Concrete," "Watching the Mevlevi *Sema* Ceremony," "Einstein's Brain," "At the Graves of my Grandparents," "Stellar Murder"

Chiron Review: "Territory," "A Rope and a Candle," "The Stuff of Stars"

East Jasmine Review (eastjasminereview.com): "Eye of a Needle," "Rogue Planet," "On Seeing Cher in Concert, Again," "Black Cat," "My Sultan," "Portrait Mask or Some Things Are Worth Waiting For"

Golden Streetcar: "At the Grave of Edvard and Nina Grieg," "*Brokeback Mountain, (2005)*"

Incandescent Mind: *Selfish Work*: "Inscape: A Poem for My Little Self"

Intersections: "Colors of Cuba"

Lummox: "A Death in the Family," "Waving, Not Drowning"

Mojave River Review: "To a Ring-tailed Lemur"

Poetry Nook: "Before I Go"

Redshift: "For Love Alone," "Saint John on Patmos"

Sheila-Na-Gig online (sheilanagigblog.com): "Balm in the Cuban Night"

Short Poems Ain't Got Nobody To Love: "The Now, or Nothing at All"

Silver Birch Press (silverbirchpress.wordpress.com): "Clifton"

Snorted the Moon & Doused the Sun: An Anthology of Addiction Poetry: "True Love," "The Day Elvis Died"

Spectrum: "Green Light"

Spilt Ink Blog (spiltinkpoetrypress.wordpress.com): "Safe Space"

Then & Now: Conversations with Old Friends: "It Has Happened"

Tofu Ink Arts Press: "Just Keep Swimming"

Also by Clifton Snider

Poetry
Jesse Comes Back (1976)
Bad Smoke   Good Body (1980)
Jesse and His Son (1982)
Edwin: A Character in Poems (1984)
Blood & Bones (1988)
Impervious to Piranhas (1989)
The Age of the Mother (1992)
The Alchemy of Opposites (2000)
Aspens in the Wind (2009)
Moonman: New and Selected Poems (2012)
The Beatle Bump (2016)

Fiction
Loud Whisper (2000)
Bare Roots (2001)
Wrestling with Angels: A Tale of Two Brothers (2001)
The Plymouth Papers (2014)

Literary Criticism
*The Stuff That Dreams Are Made On: A Jungian Interpretation of
    Literature* (1991)

Contents

Stuff of Stars

Waving, Not Drowning

Einstein's Brain

You Can't Go Home

Icons

Before I Go

STUFF OF STARS

Eye of a Needle

Persistence is not the answer,
writing here with a blanket
doubled over my knees,
no answer to the vile disturbance
brewing in your blood,
disturbance that makes you utter
terrible untrue pronouncements,
words you may or may not believe,
words that mar like superglue.

Would I could have slipped
that membrane over you,
guarded you from hunger so strong
it pushed its way
through the eye of a needle,
dying to get to heaven.

ONE LOVE

I turn to corpuscles
of the heart,
stronger than my brain,
vulnerable:
looking into my other's eyes,
the corpuscles become
tiny fireworks like blooming flowers
over the Queen Mary;
a planet circles
two suns,
two others in
regions of deep space,
and I choose love.

Can the heart choose to love
more than one at a time?
Can one, and only one,
orchid bloom in my patio
over the months
of spring & summer?

Tiny pulses
tell me harmony is possible,
music is available,
music of the spheres.

Nurtured, orchids will blossom,
music will vibrate,
a planet will turn to love,
impossible love:
fiber & fragment & tone.

Territory

A praying mantis
bright green
with fat abdomen
comes from the direction
of our neighbor's orange tree,
struggles in prickly
six-leg steps
as if the pavement
of our driveway
burns her delicate
powerful feet.

My partner gives her
a piece of notepad paper
for transport.
She startles us
with her immediate agility
to skitter across and under
the paper.

This is a predator that eats
other insects, little reptiles,
hummingbirds,
her own mate
as they procreate.

We try again,
succeed,
put her into a bush,

hydrangea,
in the back yard

among the leaves,
the green, brown-fringed leaves,
home again.

BLACK CAT

I go out to collect
the morning paper.
In the front yard,
feet from the paper,
I recognize a fellow mammal:
small residue of black fur,
cat head facing grass, red bone, paws,
no other remains
above a swarm of ants,
their goal
to eat the dead,
this black cat,
one of the skinny ones, I suppose,
I've seen prowling the back yard,
catching birds,
his turn now to be prey
of some raccoon, unleashed dog,
coyote: just that.

We bundle him away.

It Has Happened

Yes, you arrived
nineteen years ago.
Together we plumbed
the recesses of love and disease
hitherto unexplored,
unanticipated,
dark as a shut garage:
ash from a barbecue
smears the floor,
a noose hangs from the rafter;
ink burns my guts
like a fresh tattoo,
like a poem by Sylvia Plath:
the bleak descent
into insanity or death,
earthquake in Nepal,
avalanche on Everest,
a heap of snow,
a collapse of brick and wood,
body and spirit crushed,
dark as Lake Baikal,
Siberian water
20 million years old; blind fish
with no color scud along the floor.

Now That He's Gone

My ex adopted and named him Rocky
without consulting me:
Rocky, the nip and snip
long-haired orange outdoor cat
he liked to brush,
the one he threatened
to bring into the house,
the one our gray tuxedo, Lucy,
screeched at,
a screech loud as a burglar alarm.
She fought through the screen door
till she tore the mesh from its frame.

Rocky still comes round
each morning,
sleeps near the same door,
the one whose window
my ex pushed me through
in a drunken rage.

Rocky waits on the bricks
of the patio floor.
I bring him food & water,
pet him when my morning back
is not too stiff,
brush him too.
He comes to the screen
and Lucy arches her back
and screams
and I make him go away.

A Death in the Family

When the deluge struck
you took to your single bed,
installed in your room
like a comfortable coffin.
You lay down in the dark,
Soundscape on the TV.
You hoped somehow to
fade away, placid,
done with life at 38.

I said I knew how you felt
(I had been there myself).
You dismissed my words
like the books you never read,
the ones I dedicated to you.

I did not mind: I had you,
had you for more than
nineteen years. No,
for seventeen and a half
before the deluge swept away
your HIV meds, before you
consumed alcohol to smear away
the pain, made the house
your prison shared with our cats
and me.
              Then the deluge
swelled from the garage, to the driveway,
to the kitchen, till I had to escape,

escape the roiling beast
who spits invectives at the man
he used to love, who shoves him
through doors and into windows.

The deluge surges as I try to move
your car so I can escape,
as I run into another
and you take the storm outside,
to the street,
try to engulf our neighbor
till his husband calls the cops,
to whom I tell the truth,
and I watch as they handcuff you
for all the world to see,
and you die in front of me,
my last glimpse, T-shirt
stained with food and booze,
hair frayed with no baseball hat,
no ID except your phone,
and you call eleven times that night
and I say no, no, no every time,
and I leave you with love
only a longtime companion knows
and does not know.

TOUGH LOVE

I.

We cried, the pair of us,
our last cat of three in my lap
as the doctor put her down.

We acquired other cats,
rescued them from whatever fates
await the abandoned.
One is a darter.
I keep her inside,
safe from disease,
automobiles, &
bigger predators.

II.

You said it yourself:
nothing lasts forever.
You meant to die,
to abandon me,
a thing I would never abide
till now, now you've let
one of your fatal diseases
—fueled by poison in a can
or a bottle—
turn yourself from
Jekyll into Hyde,
tears into blood in
black infested eyes
one too many times and
I had to let you go.
I had to let you go.

Broken Glass

Somewhere my lover
from 1980-82
is weeping because David Bowie
is dead.
            He hung a framed poster
of the picture of Bowie on *Low*:
black hoodie, multiple shades of orange—
his hair, the orange, yellow, and black
clouds around him.
                        "Breaking Glass"
was my favorite song from that LP.

Strange
how broken glass depicts
the nature of that relationship
and figures in the end
of my late, long partnership
with a man who was
one
when the song was written.

You can replace broken glass
but you can't glue it back together
again.

True Love

My GPS guides me through
unknown territory,
undeveloped landscape of rugged
Southern California hills,
San Gabriel Valley,
clotted with townhouses
packed tight,
and I hear a Cole Porter song
on my iPod,
"True Love,"
sung by Elton John & Kiki Dee.

Why does his image
penetrate my mind?

Some layer of my nervous system,
some portion of my brain,
some muscle
—call it my heart—
belongs to him.

He was my "happy place"
when the dentist drilled
or the surgeon cut,
when we looked to each other,
by turns embraced on the bed,
and I ignored the stench of liquor
on his breath, malady
that poisoned our togetherness,

twisted and strangled
his brain cells,
sullied but did not kill
my heart,
my stubborn heart.

El Destino

Somewhere my ex-partner
of nineteen years
is weeping in his cups
over the death of Juan Gabriel
as am I, sober these many years,
listening on YouTube to "*El Destino*,"
Gabriel's sweet, sentimental duet
with Rucío Dúrcal,
both gone now.

Together we watched their concert
on video at a Mexican restaurant
in Lakewood, California—New Mexican
they falsely advertised.

My ex chastised me
for using Gabriel's "*Querida*"
on my answering machine—
why, I don't recall. The song
should have been called, "*Querido*,"
so I thought. I saw him once
at Hollywood's French Market.
He wore a bright red sweater
and sat with his posse. The bus boy
was surprised I knew who he was.

"*Mira mi solidad*"—
Look at my loneliness
the lyric goes: Look
at *his* loneliness—a closeted queer

in a homophobic culture,
as was my ex, laying floors
in shopping malls and hospitals,
disc jockey at home
and in our early years
at gay Latino parties,
till the tiny monsters
inside him grew
feeding like a hungry
bear, producing tears
I could not quell,
nightmares I could not see,
hands that pushed me away,
drinking himself into a well
nobody could reach,
least of all me.

A Rope and a Candle
for Mario

There was a time
when the image
of my body
hanging from a rope
under a beam
in my living room
brought comfort to my brain

or was it my heart—
the part that found relief
in the thought of stopping it,—
no more pain & suffering.

I was not smart enough
to make a proper noose,
one that would not slip apart,
one that snapped the neck
when the props were toppled.

He was that smart,
the man I counted on
around the house
to fix the things that broke,
the man I slept with
long after coupled bliss
became a slow, dying flame.
We lay on the bed together
to watch our favorite shows.
He favored *I Love Lucy* on DVD,

our cats he named, Lucy & Pepé,
companions more to us
than to each other.

I lit romantic candles,
we held hands,
he played too rough with Pepé,
who preferred my body to his.
Against my wishes
he took them outside.

His slow, alcoholic suicide
became visible:
ashes from a barbecue he bought,
a noose hanging in the garage.

He shoved me as if my body
was an obstacle that oppressed,
shoved my body through a window
as if to rid his troubled self
from my years of sober living.

I lit a candle for the *tres leches*
birthday cake he wanted,
surrounded by his sister,
her husband, their two daughters,
who took him away
when the fire of his rages
threatened to stifle me.

Three years passed
as he stripped himself

of car, job, family,
last vestiges of dignity,
his only friend cheap liquor
he drank to kill his pain
until only a rope
could end his troubles
forever.

In a foreign country
the news comes in a text
from his niece.

In Casablanca I discover
its only living church,
a grotto outside,
a statue of the Virgin Mary
to the left of the open door.
I light a candle.
I say a prayer.

A rope no longer comforts me.

THE STUFF OF STARS

Your eyes were like sweet, dark honey
      When I saw you at the bar that night,
      A vision of muscles and might.
Twenty-one with your own money

To buy your own drink at the bar,
      A drink to bless, curse our meeting,
      The best I could offer, a greeting.
That night you drove your sister's car

To my house and we went to bed,
      Beginning of all our bedding,
      Private, hallowed like a wedding,
Like a rose that unfolded red.

The alchemy of opposites—
      I wrote it to extol our love:
      A balm like manna from above,
A bond so real it never quits.

Your pain made self-inflicted scars,
      Asphyxiated by a rope,
      Good-bye to torment and to hope.
Our love is now the stuff of stars.

WAVING, NOT DROWNING

WAVING, NOT DROWNING

Glasses removed, I find myself
in the warm Mediterranean,
struggling to follow my French friend
to a distant buoy.

In daylight I saw it. I know it's there.
Now all is a wet blur.
I pivot to touch a bottom
I can not reach.

My panic meter rises: numbers
zoom to danger levels.
My body will not float;
it bobs like a dinghy.

My heart hurts.
I am waving,
not drowning, not yet.

I stroke to city lights—
the nearest boulders
cut feet & palms.

I press my toes into sand,
into lumpy, lovely sand.

My Sultan

Clicking my cursor on the word
"send" sets my feet,
garbed in the finest mother-made leather,
on the high wire
of a secret, sacred meeting:
mysterious eyes,
alive,
dark & deep
as feet thrust under desert sand
in the land of Mecca.

Only a micro-moment
on a lifeline
this summit of opposite worlds.

Not for all my timid eyelashes
would I have missed it:
glimpse of your culture,
accent, beard,
lips of your people from the other
side of the planet, —
no regrets, my sultan,
no regrets under a second
new moon.

Watching the Mevlevi *Sema* Ceremony

TV introduced me:
the whirling *semazens* —
men in white, full-length skirts
swirling in gentle circles, circles
within circles within circles,
the physical transformation into spirit
in a marvel of mystical space.

I looked for the young, handsome ones
and found them, dancing into ecstasy.
I saw their conical hats,
hats that symbolize their
tombstones. Black cloaks
they shed are their tombs and the white
skirts their shrouds. In circles
they march. They greet each other
soul to soul. They cross their arms:
unity of one God.
                    Today
as I watch, I see ten clean-shaven
men with two other superiors:
the Sheikh, standing for the Prophet,
sitting at his post in the back,
chanting, bowing in prayer, and another,
the bearded one, kisses the seated one
and walks among the swirling circles like a mentor
among a swarm of holy suppliants,
who seek only peace and connection,
lovers of each other and of us who watch.

Like a servant one of them kisses
his fellow *semazens* and their cloaks,

covers them at ceremony's end
as they sit in preordained fashion
in a circular room of many levels.

From the start I listen
(for *sema* means to listen, to hear)
as the man in the balcony stands, intones verses
from the Qur'an and Rumi, and the others,
all in black robes and conical hats, make music,
and I listen for what I've come to hear:
ney, the flute, oldest instrument,
symbol of divine breath of life.

Below this sacred band of men
are dervishes, head leaning right,
right hand raised up
in prayer toward heaven,
left hand facing the earth—gentle tilt
of giving what they receive from God
to the people: melding the opposites
this moment of utter serenity.

Here there is no male, no female,
or rather there is a circle of both,
dissolving differences, whirling away
wishes, pain, pleasure, ties to
the physical world, the magical flight,
via dance, to the ordered ecstasy
that spins every thing into one.

Istanbul
— 15 July 2012

35

ISTANBUL

Sober for decades,
I never expected alcohol,
a small glass of muddy brown liqueur,
served on a plate with Turkish coffee,
or an imposing bottle of red wine
on the desk in my hotel room,
in my face,
unlike the mini-bar hidden
in the fridge under the desk,
nor walls of bottled booze
displayed in windows more brazen
than any American liquor store.

Nor did I expect dolphins
in the Bosporus
where my Viking ancestors
sailed & for once
turned back,
repelled by Byzantine force.

Hagia Sophia, the Blue Mosque,
the Rustem Pasha Mosque,
where men (& women in a separate corner)
bow in prayer among tile so blue
they fix the inner eye with pleasure,
not unlike the rivers of young men,
with names like Ozgun, Ali, & Taha,
and others on Istiklal, promenade
that never quits.

A protest for prisoners of conscience
in Taksim Square,
tourists asking what it means,
snapping pictures with iPhone & iPad,
merging into the promenade,
past the Haci Baba Ottoman Restaurant,
past Starbucks & former embassies,
past medieval Galata Tower,–
a fluid wonderland of street performers,
elastic ice cream twirlers,
well-fed street cats, and, yes,
sewer stink
from time to time.

A broadcast call to prayer
on a red-hot Friday afternoon;
outside a crowded mosque
men line the sidewalk
standing, bowing in prayer
on carpet, on cardboard.

A Turkish bath,
a scrubbing followed by waves of foam
like a warm blanket
& a deep massage
by a muscled masseur
to soothe my aching calves & thighs,
to bathe my body in oil
fit for a sultan.

To a Ring-tailed Lemur

What does it mean
to encounter you,
a wild animal
among your fellows,
caged at the Jardin Zoologique
in the south of France?

I expected toucans,
depicted on either side of the entrance.
Hornbills,
from another side of the world,
live here now,
similar yet entirely different from toucans,
as are you to me,
far from your home in Madagascar,
your bright eyes,
like brown globes with pupils
framed in black and white,
dart like your fingers to search for food,
refusing to stay still
for my camera.

They transfix me,
take me back to our common home,
Africa,
millions and millions
of years ago.

Voodoo Bone Lady

Voodoo Bone Lady,
ample black woman
with ample red headdress,
guides a tour through St. Louis Cemetery,
where 100,000 bodies have decayed
in a single city block,
Voodoo Queen Marie Laveau among them,
the X's white-washed from her tomb.
(Turn around to the right three times
& make a wish, a positive wish, says the Lady.
I do.)

Here *Easy Rider* was filmed,
cameras protect from grave robbers,
and Nicholas Cage has reserved
a million-dollar pyramid
for his final home.

Walk out backwards
and throw a kiss to the right,
Voodoo Lady says,
to keep the spirits contained.
I do.

New Orleans
— 28 March 2015

BLUE ALASKA

No one expected blue skies,
no need for gloves & scarf,
no need for knitted hat.

Dormant volcano
Mount Edgecumbe stands
like a twin of Mount Fuji, —
slight streaks of snow
on its crest
punctuate a cloudless blue sky
above calm waters
of Sitka Sound,
almost tropical blue.

From Hoonah, Tlingit village,
a helicopter ride
over blue ocean inlets.
Tree covered islands
framed in turquoise.

From the air we see pools
of pure blue water,
ice melting in the sun
on Mendenhall Glacier,
mysterious as the moon;
granite & red rocks
iron laden
lie scattered,
carried by the ice slowly

to the sea, crevices
fifteen feet and deeper,
with clear blue pristine water.

Melting ice we walk on
glistens, a patina:
blue on white ice
splattered with black specks
and single deciduous leaves
imprinted as in a frame
or a 19th-century book:
the beauty of decay
amidst the blue of Alaska.

Balm in the Cuban Night
for Jorge Luis

We sit on the concrete wall
marked in black graffiti—
Havana's *Malecón*.
The lighthouse of el Castillo del Morro
beams a single light
behind us
at twilight.
Arms around each other,
we pose for the camera:
compelling, deep brown skin
glows with inner light,
smile of a model from
Santiago de Cuba
next to the older poet,
pale with skin alight,
and gray mustache.

Lightning flashes in the distance
over the city
beyond construction cranes.
He warns of the cannon boom,
from the castle,
thunder in the dark
at 9 o'clock,
remnant of Spanish rule
call to curfew,
and so it blasts
and we take our walk;

smartphone lights the way
to a ride together
in the back seat of a 50's
Dodge convertible,
red as the blind blood
flooding my heart,
emerging magic
and mystery,
cubano y americano
making some kind of music
in the balm of the night.

Colors of Cuba

The 1950's cars,
pride of their owners
more than a wife
says our guide—
they recall my 1955 used Oldsmobile,
first car, gift from my parents.
I painted it turquoise,
drove it off to college,
neglected to give it water,
cracked the block.

No Cuban maestro mechanic to fix it then.

A joy to ride in the back seat of a convertible Dodge
or Ford, to hold hands at night in the back seat of a 1950 Chevy
with my dark-skinned *amigo cubano*.

The colors of the cars are transcendent—
candy apple red, chartreuse,
other shades of green & blue,
hot pink, yellow, white,
orange, lavender—
whatever the tropical mind
imagines.

The Cuban men, they told me,
are gorgeous
(the women too, I suppose—
I have my biases)—

palates of Spain, Africa, Anglo, Indian.
They did not lie.

The tops of the buildings crumble in Havana.
No one fixes them,
dirt-dark streets are home to
stray dogs and cats skinny enough
to slip through parted wood
to escape a Cuban cooking pot.

The failed revolution is advertised on billboards
with ubiquitous copies
of that Korda photo, world-famous:
their national murderous thug,
Che Guevara.

Ubiquitous too are rum & cigars & live music—
salsa, mambo, rumba,
Guantanamera,
Michael Jackson & The Beatles,
banned for so many years.

Pink plumerias
& other lavender flowers
at the Hemingway House.

The books of Reynaldo Arenas
—queer Cuban writer who died of AIDS
in New York decades ago—
are still *prohibido*.
At Fábrica de Arte Cubano

two *viejas* kiss on the lips
in a painting,
two *viejos* embrace in bed
and the paintings of persecuted queer Cuban artists
hang in El Museo Nacional de Bellas Artes,
bleak reminders of the pre-and-post Castro past.

The sun is coming out in Cuba,
hot as a hammer & wet as blood,
melting barriers erected
long ago
now crumbling
like the gray walls of buildings
waiting to be repaired.

EXCURSION

I spend my time ashore
in Quintana Roo,
the Yucatán, Mexico,
in a rain forest
among the Chacchoben
Mayan Ruins,
where delicate yellow and maroon
orchids grow,
where blue morpho butterflies
flit across the trails,
where spider monkeys
prowl the trees,
where fer-de-lance
and other poison snakes dwell,
where a strangler fig
hugs a hapless palm,
where men were sacrificed,
painted blue,
on the top of the pyramid —
the winner of a race
(savior to his people)
and prisoners of war
and children
and Spanish missionaries,
their hearts cut out,
not so glad to lay their heads
on the altar of stone.
My friend and I touch stones
on the ancient pyramid
and I connect

at once
with the ancient ones,
with the moss on the stones,
with the forest
and its creatures,
and my fellow travelers, —
all of us one
in this single, luminous moment.

At the Grave of Edvard and Nina Grieg

Their names are carved large,
sidewise
bold and crude
in a dolmen
embedded in a cliff-sized rock
surrounded by Norwegian birch,
white and pink flowers
in woods inhabited by trolls
and tourists,—
it faces the sprawling lake
with its islands
covered evergreen
in the exact spot
where the sun hit
on an afternoon
and the composer of *Peer Gynt*
said, "When I die,
put me there."

Troldhaugen, Norway
—19 July 2017

BRIDE

Thor loses his hammer,
the one that always returned
like a boomerang,
that always hit its mark.

The giant who stole the hammer
promises to give it back
if the Nordic gods give him to marry
the most beautiful woman they have.

Thor & Loki, demonic
trickster, dress as women,
Thor as the beautiful bride
with a veil to cover his beard.

They journey
to the country of the giants,
are welcomed with mead
and tables of bounteous food.

And when the hammer is
produced, Thor takes it
and smashes the giant
and all his fellows at the court.

ICELAND WITH A COLD

I.

The weather is nasty cold
as I sit in the tour bus
pockets packed with tissues.
We stop at a geothermal plant
where a volcano
heats water piped to Reykjavík—
Ring of Fire they call it.

I don't care about the explanations.
To be here is enough:
to see a geyser spout,
a memory of Old Faithful,
over fifty years ago,
to see a spreading plant
of yellow flowers,
its broad leaves wealthy
with drops of water
from steaming pools.

Thingvellir,
National Park,
has a rift—evidence of
continents colliding,
and the first parliament
in the world, 930 A.D.,
dense with fog
this cold and weary day.

In Reykjavík six-sided glass panes
embroider the Harpa Theater
where tonight I sniffle through
proud poems of Halldór Laxness
set into "Pearls of Icelandic Songs,"
pianist, soprano, and baritone.

II.

Next day on the bus into town
I hear a father & son make plans
to visit the Viking Museum.
I ask to tag along, listen to the father
talk of his business and cheap air fare,
far from the foundation of a Viking long house
well over a thousand years old.

My goal is the tallest building in the country:
the church majestic on a hill with the sculpture
of the Viking hero, Leif Eriksson,
who reached the New World
500 years before Columbus,
who my childish mind imagined
could be my ancestor.

III.

Near Akureyri in the north, our guide
sings to us as we travel through a sunlit valley
with green hills, horses, sheep, round bails of hay
wrapped in colored plastic: pink, blue, black, white,
where, she tells us, live elves & trolls.

But no more Nordic gods. Odin, Thor, Freya,—
all tossed into the splendiferous water falls,
Godafoss, a thousand years ago.

For the moment my cold has disappeared.

The Monument to the Unknown Bureaucrat (1993),
Magnús Tómasson

The sculpture of a man
stands on cobblestones
near the chill water
of Tjörnin, Reykjavík.

Rain clouds
part in the distance,
open a pale blue sky,
green grass & trees
on the other side,
a church to the far left,
its white & green-gray steeple
topped by a weather vane.

Icelandic seagulls
white & gray feathers,
yellow & red-dotted beaks,
float and fly over the City Hall
nearby.

A gray briefcase hangs from
the right hand of the man
in a green-gray business suit
and rumpled shoes.

Oblivious to the life
around him,
a block of volcanic rock

more than twice his size
obliterates his head & shoulders.

At his feet:
a mess of
votive candles.

Reykjavík, Iceland
— 22 July 2017

RIB Ride, Geiranger Fjord, Norway

We are twelve, bundled
in yellow & blue inflated suits
as if we were going to the moon.

Glasses over glasses,
smartphone & Nikon at the ready,
I take a seat in the front row,
assisted by a blond god
whose name
I learn later,
is Lukas,
my temporary *Bel Ami*.

Our young Norwegian guide
with reflector glasses
stops to tell of the farmers
half way up the cliff
and how the children sailed
to school.

We veer and bump
into willing water
to the Viking Age
and the Seven Sisters falls
with their Suitor
across from them,
who offers a bottle of wine
they wisely reject. His water
wets our faces as the boat

comes close enough to kiss
and then we speed on
for a look at his rival:
a giant face in solid rock
with empty eyes, a knocked off nose
and a frown, a sad, sad frown,
frozen in the mythic North.

At the boat house
I talk to Lukas,
a Czech who wants to bike
Seattle to Southern California
and, if the gods comply,
to my house,
and into my own
personal myth.

STONEHENGE

Gray sky
& black birds on the
bright green grass,
& red poppies
& white daisies
pop from the soil,
and now, this very day,
we humans watch
and marvel
and document
with zoom lens cameras
and smartphones.

We mill around
in solemn joy—
witnesses
to a world-class
celebrity
in stupendous isolation,
massive stones
erect
and lying atop
the others
or on the ground—
a mute, mutilated
mandala,
Earth-bound,
moss-covered,
majestic.

The wet sky assaults,
completes the circle
for a single day.

FOR LOVE ALONE
for Achraf

I.

Tagine-prepared
vegetables, lamb, chicken, sardines,
olives of all colors and kinds, dates,
mint tea, "Moroccan whiskey."
White pomegranates, oranges, yogurt.
Majoun.
Kif—stuff for poets & writers
of the fifties & sixties.

Camel boys of the desert,
divine night,
a sand dune & the numinous
Milky Way, the panoply of stars.

II.

I have come for him,
my cyber lover,
his mass of black hair, exploding, shaved
on the side in the current fashion, commanding
masculine hair.

The living package that
wraps the waves of his hard abdomen,
the muscles of his arms and legs: all this,—
erastes and *eromenos*.

All this and to thank me for visiting his country,
he draws my name in green & red Moroccan Arabic
and sends a picture of himself holding it, his face
the face I love, the deep dark eyes,
deep with the mysteries of a continent,
the wisdom of youth, the full, perfect lips
I cannot taste for fear of king & country,
of triples of soldiers & cops holding
automatic rifles on corners of Casablanca,
terrorists against those like us
whose only crime is love.

Survivor (The Killing Fields)

The bones are stacked
like broken bamboo,
the skulls stare mute
as if picked clean
by a black & white bird.

Chickens meander,
cocks crow. Palm trees,
plumeria, a peacock, bright grass
on little grave mounds,
plots empty of their bodies.

Memorial for gentle
men with glasses,
smart women, boys & girls,
stripped of their clothes.

I place a yellow
chrysanthemum
and a stick of incense.
I pose for a picture

with an 88-year-old
survivor, hug him,
say with candor,
"God bless you."

Phnom Penh, Cambodia
— 3 October 2019

EINSTEIN'S BRAIN

O My Flora

Not you in the garden,
you whom I dearly love,
cultivate, prune, water, feed:
roses, orchids, bromeliads,
amaryllis, bella donna,
purple/red/pink/white geraniums,
California poppies,
angel's trumpets, yellow
& double-fluted white,
brilliant orange-red hibiscus,
faithful irises, my fruit trees;
epiphyllum and other cacti,
palm and other trees,
oleanders, poisonous
to the mouth
like the angel's trumpets.

No, not you, my dear ones, and
all the others I've forgot.
This poem is for the one
hundred trillion microbes
—tenfold more than my body cells—
who inhabit my corpus,—bacteria,
generations of yeast, virus, amoeba,
& fungus I have fought & lived with
these many years since I emerged
from my mother's womb.

Thank you for helping me chump my food,
flush it out with your own departed,

fight off sick-making organisms.

Forgive me for killing you by accident
with medicine from my doctor,
for bathing my hair, my entire surface
to kill those who would do harm.

Nevermind, at the end of time (our time)
we will burn, destroy one cycle,
begin another.

STELLAR MURDER

From what I'm told
the tiniest particle
in my living cells
resembles the architecture
of the universe;
a swooping image of bright orange & red
against solid black
generated by a computer
illustrates a black hole
two billion years ago
slowly sucking in a dying star
caught
too close to the hungry hole
caught
in a tidal disruption,—
only
there is no moon,
no tide going out,
only the bleak darkness
of a galaxy
found in space
and a star
that is no more.

Portrait Mask or
Some Things Are Worth Waiting For

Our adolescent cats
would delight to paw and tear
strands of cedar bark & feathers
on my First Nation Portrait Mask
hanging above the piano, bold
in red and black on red cedar.

I remove the mask,
place it high as I can
above DVDs, CDs, old cassettes
in my media closet, where,
door closed, Pepé and Lucy,
especially Lucy, star jumper
who reached the top of the frig,
will not disturb the portrait:
a man with a younger man
on his forehead—"He's got him
on his mind," said the artist
from Vancouver Island
at the Southwest Museum.

Pepé and Lucy scrabble,
thump
the hardwood floors.

The portrait stares
at the ceiling, waits
to be back in place.

Rogue Planet

A telescope in Hawaii
spies a unique planet
floating in the Milky Way
—first of its kind—
no orbit,
no sun or star
to warm it, keep it
steady,
       alone,
an orphan
in cold space,
circumference circled by
swirling mauve & white waves,
drifting,
no place to go,
no one to care,
except scientists,
looking for "failed stars,"
"brown dwarfs": they discover
this solitary planet,
this rogue
out there somewhere,
a mere eighty light years away,
roaming into
human imagination:
a purple circle
six times larger than Jupiter,
it wanders
alone
in the dark.

Einstein's Brain

He played Mozart on the violin
& stuck his long tongue out
for the camera,
hair flying and flopping
like synapses gone wild.

Icon of genius,
brain bigger than usual,
he left it to science
to be sliced into minute detail,
parsed and purloined and now
nearly 60 years after he died
scientists say he had an enormous
corpus callosum.
                    Long & generous,
well endowed for any man,
young or old,
it reached from his forehead to nape,
pulsed with electrical messages
from right to left brain,
creative synergy,
the truth of yoga
—balance—
his truth.

GREEN LIGHT

Morning meditation:
in darkness of my closed eyes
I see a field of green light.

Today a surgeon
pierces my left eyelid
with a needle—tears gush;
the medicine is bitter
on my throat. The surgeon
places a black contact lens
on my left eye, performs her
delicate business, removes
a growth on my upper lid.
Under the white cover over my face
I shut my right eye
as she cuts, cauterizes.
I smell burnt flesh &
from the upper right side
of my covered eye
a green light flashes,
a floating rectangle
a beam of hope.

The Now, or Nothing at All

Only scientists
could name a galaxy
EGS-zs8-1
13.1 billion light-years from us,
born 675 million years after
the Big Bang
(current creation myth).

Three telescopes
assembled the picture:
a blue-white splotch
surrounded by a darker blue aura,
then total black.

Further than any other galaxy
yet discovered,
it may, in this present moment,
be dead,
dissolved to invisible matter,
or nothing,
nothing at all.

Big Hole

Scientists have discovered
a fossil
540 million years old
size of a grain of sand,
one millimeter,
ancestor of humans,
a deuterostome
with a giant mouth,
eight cone-like openings
four on either side
and no anus.

This tiny creature
with an enormous maw
spawned sea urchins,
starfish,
all manner of vertebrates,
like us
with our hungry
clean & filthy
human
holes.

EASY DOES IT

Yesterday the heart doctor
diagnosed mine:
"premature ventricular beats,"
he said, as if my heart
were racing to reach
its allotted number.

My visceral metronome
is fine till I get up
in the morning.
My monkey brain chatters.
I hear it
during unsuspected moments—
at work in my garden,
doing cardio at the gym,
hearing unwanted news.

Age has swollen a corner
of my heart and weakened
its lower chambers,
the ones that push blood
into my lungs and arteries,
and I have no idea
how many beats remain
nor do I want to know.

YOU CAN'T GO HOME

At the Graves of My Grandparents

I hunt through Greenwood Cemetery,
Superior, Wisconsin,
with my first cousin, once removed,
for graves of my English-Canadian
grandfather & my Norwegian grandmother,
parents of my mother.

Mosquitoes are pesky;
we go on, row by row.

Michael finds the place—
two modest markers: Norman C. Tout,
Henrietta Tout. Always
a comforting relief,
not a pleasure,
to find what you're looking for
in a graveyard.

Mosquitoes—the biting females—
are happy to find us there.
They swarm into a fury,
attacking as if we had
no business to honor
our human ancestors.

I snap pictures, pause for a prayer
& we flee as if from a Greek
pestilence.

FINDING THE TOUT HOUSE

Google is no help
nor is the GPS on my phone,
to find the house on 1st Avenue East,
the one house on that portion of the street,
in Superior, Wisconsin—a house I know
from my child and teen years
& countless snapshots of Mom, posing
like a movie star with her
Mary Pickford curls, oldest of four,
sitting as a little girl
on the porch steps with her Norwegian
grandmother, the only picture we have of her,
other pictures with white borders of Mother
with her two sisters and one brother,
her mother & father.
                              Yes
I know this house with a bathroom
upstairs, bedrooms on either side
with slanted ceilings, the kitchen,
changed forever now,
where my grandmother baked
delicate powdered Norwegian pastries.

Distant neighbors provide options
on where this house might be;
I remember adjacent railroad tracts
& by testing different routes
we find the house at last.

Green Bay Packer signs,
human-sized depictions
of Minnie Mouse, Popeye & Olive Oil, and
numerous other frolicsome figures & banners
decorate the house, lawn, garage, sheds.
Reminders of California, my home.

A deer crosses a backyard three times
bigger than my own. We poke around,
taking pictures till we find the present keepers
sitting behind the house sipping afternoon drinks
on a perfect June day.
                        Steward of the house
for thirty years, the man inquires,
"Are you Touts?" and I know
we are home at last.

You Can't Go Home

I.

I return to the home he provided
when I was 9 & 10
at the same age my preacher dad
died.
      Fifty-six years have passed.
An African American preacher & son
—with their wives—keep the two-story
plus basement
parsonage,
made of red brick like the church next door,
pristine—
green Indiana grass.
The only section smaller
than I expected is the lawn
between church & driveway
where I learned to hate
dog shit.

II.

Hours of tedious violin practice
in my upstairs back bedroom,
shared with a brother 13 months younger,
different from me as chalk to coal dust.

Across the hall—our older brother,
rebellious in leather jacket

& hidden cigarettes,
suffered weeks from poison ivy.

III.

The younger preacher's wife
opens the sanctuary next door,
air conditioned now.
I remember hot Sunday morning services
with fans waving haphazard
and a demon dressed like an evangelist
who preached on Sunday night
against the "unpardonable sin"
and shoved a brier seed in my gut
that grew to my heart
into a choking bush
as we moved from the parsonage
to a house my father built across town
to a series of houses in California
till he built another one
just like it, only reversed,
where I learned to trust the Lord
to stifle the temptation, the fear,
to burn the brier to nothing.

This took a little while.

ICONS

ON SEEING CHER IN CONCERT, AGAIN

She calls herself an icon now,
one step above diva.
When we were teens
she was simply a hero,
singing Dylan better than Dylan
when I needed a friend.
I found a boyfriend.
We played "I Got You Babe"
in my living room when no one else
was home & so tonight
when she sings the song again live
with Sonny revived
on the circular video screen,
tears arrive
and I find it hard, so hard
to raise my voice again
to a concert-level whoop
as she completes the show
in her other costumes,
always the same persona:
neglected goddess
who rises from the foam,
who knows who she is & is proud of it,
as she breezes by on a shrine-like pedestal
in the air and sings, "I Hope You Find It."
I have, *ma chèrie*,
I have.
Merci.

CONCRETE

for Robin Williams

Layers of concrete,
rough, smoothed,
hardened
over the decades,
smothering love.
Through a small hole
the spirit gushed
like Old Faithful,
a marvel of hot reliability
his way of returning
the love.
Fun, funny, deadly serious—
the voices bubbled and burned
hiding disease (booze,
powder, Parkinson's),
the weight of cement.

Layers of concrete
cover a festered stillness,
emptiness
between the explosions. They
slowly crowd the hole,
this concrete no mason ever poured.

No way out,
the breath squeezes away
all the love.
Then stillness
and release,
the concrete
all gone.

The Day Elvis Died

I walk home from the beach
to my upstairs apartment,
Long Beach, 16 August 1977.
The cute sailor next door
appears on the balcony,
tells me Elvis Presley has died.

I'm dead tired from teaching
remedial English, hung over,
four hours every morning
at the local community college.

The radio & TV stations play
almost exclusively one song,
"Are You Lonesome Tonight,"
between the known details
of his dying, as if it were
his most representative
& appropriate song,
with his melodramatic
spoken voice about the world
as a stage where love is lost,
a poignant interlude,
an introduction to the grave.

Drunk that I am,
a year before sobriety,
I attempt to save the moment,
record from the radio

on my cassette tape recorder
till it jams while I am passed out.

Next morning, head throbbing,
dehydrated, drained,
I face a room of domestic
& foreign students.
They don't mind that I play
what I could save from my tape:
"Are You Lonesome Tonight."

SAINT JOHN ON PATMOS

By the River Jordan
I saw the Holy Spirit
descend like a dove
& hover over his head.

I knew then I would follow him
to the end. We bonded in love,
inhaled the fragrance that comes
from a hidden heavenly marriage.

My older brother, James,
has been dead
these fifty years, martyr
to King Herod's sword.

I preached in Ephesus,
was sent to Rome.
There the Emperor
dropped my body into a vat
of boiling oil. By grace
my flesh was not harmed.

I was banished here
to the mountains of
the island of Patmos
in the deep blue Mediterranean.

In this cave my lord and lover
came like exploding
volcanic fire,
charging me to write his Revelations.

You, Prochorus,
my young apprentice,
with the golden hair
and the luminous face,
face like the face
of my lord, listen
to my story, how I lay
my head upon his breast,
my holy husband, when
at supper he blessed us twelve,
knowing one of us would
betray him in the Garden.

Of his disciples, I alone
stayed by the cross as
he hung in agony.
I stayed steadfast with his mother, Mary,
her sister, and Mary Magdalene.
He said to his mother,
"Woman, behold your son!" And
to me, "Behold thy mother!"
I took her to my bosom
until the day she died.

Come Prochorus, let us rest,
ponder the mystery
of God's creation.
My days are few.
I give you word
of the Apocalypse.
Pass it on until
my lord returns.

BROKEBACK MOUNTAIN (2005)

Jack and Ennis,
two sheep-herding cowboys,
gaze slyly at each other
before they find themselves
in lust and love
in a tent
on Brokeback Mountain.

Never again will they be
so whole,
so one with themselves
in the chill of the mountain
like the cowboy shirts Jack saves
one inside the other.

Just Keep Swimming

The queen clownfish
was born a male
like all the other fry.

She attends her court,
all male, among the sea
anemones. She
agitates them
so they remain male.

When she dies
the biggest male
transitions into a female,
becomes the new queen
and the cycle continues.

Before I Go

Before I Go

Give me numinous olive oil, ultra:
blood streaming, corpuscles
pulsing with sap—sweetest
maple from the north,
capillaries lubricated
with oil of Oriental palms.

Let me sip Turkish coffee
in an Arab oasis,
hold hands with a prince
under cedars of Lebanon,
savor strains of the ney,
violin crafted by a genius
in old Europe,
divine music from Songs
of Solomon, Rumi, Kama Sutra.

Let me see eternity
in a Blakean grain of sand,
Heaven in a California Poppy,
kneel before the Unseen God,
take the dust from his lotus-like
feet—incarnate image,
naked, human.
                    Feed from
his endorsement and,
complete,
fade into eternity.

SAFE SPACE

Yoga was a safe space
for an introvert like me.

The only man tonight,
I arrive late,
avoid the chatter,
content to yield
to our instructor,
a new mother.
She praises our amateur poses.

My favorites:
tadasana, mountain pose,
shavasana, corpse pose,
and final lotus pose,
hands folded, head bowed;
our teacher chants
in Sanskrit, and we finish:
namaste.

At the front desk
is a new woman, a temp.
She is missing when I return
from the men's room,
as are all the other women,
and I am locked inside the
Wellness Center, with no smartphone,
no wallet, no modern convenience
but the dead computer and the phone
at the desk.
I call 911.

SYNCHRONICITY
for Andrew Berner, 1945-2014

Infection plugs my left ear
as I step from the shower
at the moment you are drifting
into the sleep that comes to all.

My poem is unfinished when the news
arrives the next day. I wanted
to celebrate nearly forty years
of friendship. You lived a half block
from me. I used to look for your VW bug,
anticipate drinking at "Uncle" Bell's
condo on the beach, getting shit-faced
every time. Other times we'd lie in the sun
and I'd tell you how I cut back on my drinking
by using smaller glasses. We stopped at your place
and you brought out the pot. We went to San Diego
to see Shakespeare at the Globe Theatre
with your ex-lover, then to the bath house:
you offered pills like a priest
handing out wafers.

You got sober, off and on, moved away
to grad. school and clinical psychology
and permanent sobriety. I followed
when my time arrived.

I wanted to mention how
you conquered non-Hodgkin's,
suffered decades of arthritis,

your hands and feet gnarled
tighter as the years went by
like a strangler fig,
how you could not lick
a lifelong addiction to nicotine,
how you explained: "Part of me
wants to die
more than it wants to live," & I
wanted to express my rage
at the cancer that crippled your lungs,
stifled your breath.

I wanted to iterate
your spontaneous laughter,
your gentle voice—erudite, opinionated,
caring, sometimes wrong, more often
right—how we loved
many of the same things,
hung paintings by an artist
you introduced me to,
meditated at the meeting
you founded, then supped
in Laguna or Dana Point,
conversed for hours
in your condo with its ocean view
and, yes, how we shared a love of
orchids, orchids, orchids.

Today I celebrate the lotus-like postures
of synchronicity that structured
our years of friendship, a bond
only a Higher Power could forge.

CLIFTON

Growing up,
I hated my first name.
Who else was named Clifton?
It was a name apart, a name
for someone like me,
last-to-be-chosen
(football or baseball),
the boy who played violin,
an instrument girls excelled on,
a name confused with
"Clifford," clumsy
with its double f's,
a name I hated worse than my own.

In high school I worked
as bus boy at
Clifton's Cafeteria,
a reason to like my name.
I'd whip out my
driver's license to prove
to customers who I was.

I discovered Clifton Webb
in vintage movies on TV.
Perfect hair & mustache,
always proper, exquisite
suit & tie, a gentleman I assumed
was British with his eloquent
diction, covertly gay,
of course, as was I at the time,

a hero going down on the Titanic,
a comfort to his young son
he'd hitherto been estranged from,
down but not defeated —
a role model for a young queer
who did not yet own
his own exquisite self.

Inscape: A Poem for My Little Self

I looked inside myself
on a crisp March afternoon
and this is what I found:

a boy of maybe 3 1/2
in Wisconsin,
the kitchen
of his Norwegian grandmother,
in her house dress.
He looks up at the oven,
takes in the smell
of fresh baked rosettes
sprinkled with powdered sugar:
my single living memory of her.

I see myself, a little older,
playing alone
in the driveway between our church
in Joliet, Illinois,
and the house my father built.
I build a little city of clay,
brown & gray mud.

I see that boy
holding a 3/4-size violin
at his first lesson
with gray-haired Mr. Herath,
downtown Joliet,

and I see a photo of myself,
black & white,
in Terre Haute, Indiana,
posing with my violin
for a snapshot with no flash.

Carsick returning home
from our first trip to California,
I vomit bile into the toilet
in the motel,
nothing else to expel.

My father left the church in Terre Haute
to build a ranch house
in the country.
I slip through a wire fence,
wander alone
in the woods behind the house,
balance, walk
on fallen trees.

I listen to forbidden records,
45 singles, my older brother plays,
and on the radio,
light green plastic, the one
I made my parents exchange
for the microscope I'd wanted,
the one my father called a "toy."

I attend 5th grade in 5 different schools
until we settle for awhile

in La Habra, California.

                    I wander alone,
wearing a homemade superhero cape,
hoisting a wooden spear
in the fragrant orange grove
behind our house
with its neat rows of trees,
its falling white petals and
fallen fruit. (All this became
a tract of houses after we left.)

We moved to Lakewood,
left my best friend next door
behind,
my last best friend till college.

We wrestled, spent the night
in sleeping bags behind his house,
I was crazy jealous because he invited
my brother, over a year younger than me,
to go to Disneyland with us.

That best friend, that Mormon boy,
who tried to convert me
as I, the Pentecostal preacher's kid,
tried to convert him, —
these boys thrive,
frozen in a black & white
snapshot,
arms around each other,
alone
so alone.

ORLANDO

Today I grieve
for the 20-year-old
assaulted by teenagers
in Long Beach
across from the queer bar
so many years ago.

I grieve for my friends
and my ex-lover
who took pills with liquor to die,
who shot and gassed themselves.

I grieve for the countless others
who died
because a callous president
did nothing to provide
medicine and research,
to offer a safe place
to heal.

I grieve for brothers and sisters
in muggy Florida, celebrating
freedom to party, to dance,
to lust,
to love each other,
whose blood has been shed
by a man who beat his wife,
who loathed his own queer self,
who yielded to the voices

of sanctimonious hate
across the sea,

who could not bear
the sight of two men kissing
in a public park,
who purchased an AR-15
assault rifle,
a hand gun
with impunity
and practiced hate
where there was love.

Letter to the Children
Separated at the Border
from Their Families

Dear Children,

I have heard your voices on YouTube,
crying *"Papá, Papá."*
I have heard
the six-year-old girl
who begged to talk to her aunt
whose number she memorized.

You will suffer in the future.
You'll wince or cry,
when you see
corrugated fences
like the cages
border patrol put you in.
You'll shrink from men & women
in uniform, fear any adult noise,
fear the touch of their hands.

Some of you will find your families,
some may not and if you were
too little when they kidnapped you,
you may not remember your people
at all.
        While the world watches soccer
players in another country, you will play
with your new, temporary friends

as children do,
and for those moments you'll forget
the hands that forced you, that
put you down, until the time
to sleep and the uniforms,
the fences and the walls stifle
your imagination
and your spirit
yearns to rest forever.

May the bright light
of empathy,
of love & compassion,
warm your bones
make you free at last.

Roof

The roofer has come
to replace the red tile that leaked
when the rains came.

He supplies dark brown gutters
to funnel the water
when the rain comes.

Long dinge lines
mar the stucco
where the water
spilled over.

I sit inside
with my cats & my books
alone and dry
under a clear night sky.

QUARANTINE

It makes me feel
like a corner thread
in a Turkish carpet,
a web in a forgotten corner,
not a statistic,
not yet,
just a comma,
an adjective,
at best a noun
in the daily news.

About the Author

Clifton Snider is the internationally acclaimed author of eleven books of poetry, including *Moonman: New and Selected Poems* and *The Beatle Bump*, and four novels, the most recent of which is his historical novel, *The Plymouth Papers*. He pioneered LGBTQ literary studies at California State University, Long Beach. A Jungian/Queer literary critic, he has published hundreds of poems, short stories, reviews, and articles internationally, as well as the scholarly book, *The Stuff That Dreams Are Made On: A Jungian Interpretation of Literature*. He holds a Ph.D. in English literature from the University of New Mexico and retired from teaching at California State University, Long Beach, in 2009. He is the recipient of the Lorde-Whitman Award from OUT LOUD: A Cultural Evolution, 2018. His work has been translated into Arabic, French, Russian, and Spanish.